BALANCING
Blessings

Balancing Blessings

A Woman's Devotional & Prayer Guide

Sandra Miller

ByB E-Publishers, LLC
Woodbridge, VA 22191

BALANCING BLESSINGS

Copyright © 2024 by Sandra Miller

ISBN-13: 978-0-9800093-2-3
ISBN-10: 0-9800093-2-4

All rights reserved. No part of this publication may be reproduced, stored in a retrieval system, or transmitted in any form or by any means—electronic, mechanical, photocopy, recording, or any other—except for brief quotations in printed reviews without the author's prior permission.

Some of the content in this book originally appeared in the first edition of *Balancing Blessings and Obtaining Order* by Sandra Miller, published in 2008 by ByB E-Publishers under ISBN 978-0-9800093-0-9.

Unless otherwise noted, all scripture verses and quotations are taken from the following sources:

Scripture taken from the New King James Version®. Copyright © 1982 by Thomas Nelson. Used by permission. All rights reserved.

Scriptures taken from the Holy Bible, New International Version®, NIV®. Copyright © 1973, 1978, 1984, 2011 by Biblica, Inc. Used by permission of Zondervan. All rights reserved worldwide.

The "NIV" and "New International Version" are trademarks registered in the United States Patent and Trademark Office by Biblica, Inc.

Publisher/Editor/Compiler/Cover design by ByB E-Publishers, LLC
Cover photo by Sticker2You, LLC | Licensed via: stock.adobe.com
Book art by various artists, including: Sandra Miller, Hulinska Yevheniia | Licensed via: stock.adobe.com and KatyaKatya | Licensed via: stock.adobe.com

Printed in the United States of America

This book belongs to:

_____

balance blesses

Table of Contents

Author's Message — IX

Step 1: Getting Geared Up
— *Mary the Mother of Jesus* — 3

Step 2: Establishing Proper Priorities
— *Mary and Martha* — 11

Step 3: Prayerfully Planning Ahead
— *Esther* — 19

Step 4: Exercising and Eating Healthy
— *The Syro-Phoenician Woman* — 27

Step 5: Conquering Your Clutter
— *The Woman with the Alabaster Box* — 35

Step 6: Evolving through Productive Pursuits
— *Deborah* — 43

Step 7: Reviving Your Relationships
— *Abigail* — 51

Step 8: Making Your Ministry Matter
— *The Samaritan Woman* — 59

Step 9: Getting Financially Focused
— *The Prophet's Widow* — 67

Step 11: Being Divine by Design
— *Sarah* — 75

Step 12: Caring for Your Castle
　　—The Shunammite Woman   *83*

Conclusion: Keeping God Close
　　—Ruth   *91*

Introduction

Author's Message:

Have you ever considered how some challenges faced by women in an earlier era still exist today? Walk with me into the hearts, souls, and passions of women in the Bible who, through God's unconditional love and grace, found godly balance in their service to God and others.

"Balancing Blessings" is a companion book that offers insights from the Bible into the lives of twelve women who found spiritual balance by embracing the principles of grace through Jesus Christ. Each devotional examines the character qualities, roles, and relationships of women such as Mary, Esther, Deborah, Abigail, Ruth, and others. By stepping back in time and experiencing life-defining moments with these women, we see how God's unmerited favor intervened and helped them navigate life's fears, insecurities, and uncertainties. Moreover, from these women, we discover how to cultivate a more meaningful relationship with God and others and how to take steps toward obtaining spiritual balance in our own lives.

God's grace, which is unlimited in supply, is not withdrawn because of our sins, nor is it lessened. Ecclesiastes 7:20 reminds us that no one is entirely righteous and free from sin. The balance in being blessed with God's Grace is being able to receive the blessings of God for ourselves but also the willingness to share it with others.

I have organized the chapters in this devotional and prayer guide to correspond with those in its companion book: "Balancing Blessings and Obtaining Order." Quotes at the beginning of each chapter are taken from the companion book and focus on a specific topic, aligning with my eleven-step process designed to help women achieve some semblance of balance and order in every aspect of their lives—based on God's Word and Will.

In addition, each chapter contains a devotional, guided prayer, and reflection questions designed to empower women to live a life that reflects God's many blessings of forgiveness, redemption, salvation, transformation, wisdom, love, hope, joy, peace, mercy, grace, faith, etc.

My hope and prayer for you is that God's unmerited favor guides you through the challenges and uncertainties of life to find the blessings of His saving grace.

Simply Blessed, Sandra Miller

Step 1

Getting Geared Up

Magnify the Lord

LIFE IS A
BALANCING ACT,
AND HOW EFFECTIVELY WE
PERFORM—BY
HANDLING THE STRESSES
AND DEMANDS OF
EVERY DAY—IS
DIRECTLY RELATED TO
THE LEVEL OF ORDER WE
WILL HAVE IN OUR
DAY-TO-DAY LIVES.

Step 1

From the Heart of God's Woman

Mary

Read: Luke 1:26-56

Mary, the mother of Jesus, was of the lineage of David, a virgin from a poor family rich in heritage. Many women longed to be the mother of the Messiah, but God had chosen her. Let us go back through the corridor of time and imagine what it was like for Mary when she received the news that she would be the mother of Jesus Christ.

It was like lightning illuminating the room in sheer spender so bright; she had to close her eyes. Even with her eyes closed, the brightness was transparent. In the midst of the glorious light was a sound so soothing and comforting that it snatched the fear that had besieged her when the light first made its startling presence. The same sweet sound was heard again and again, each time becoming increasingly audible. "Rejoice, highly favored one, the Lord is with you; blessed are you among women!" (Luke 1:28).

She opened her eyes again and contemplated falling to her knees, but once the greeting from the angel registered in her mind and heart, she began to wonder: Who is this that I stand before? What kind of greeting did I receive? Sensing her concerns, the angel says to her, "Do not be afraid, Mary, for you have found favor with God" (v. 30).

Once the angel had noted Mary's genuine acceptance of who he was, he shared with her the reason for his visit:

> *And behold, you will conceive in your womb and bring forth a Son, and shall call His name JESUS. He will be great, and will be called the Son of the Highest; and the Lord God will give Him the throne of His father David. And He will reign over the house of Jacob forever, and of His kingdom there will be no end." Then Mary said to the angel, "How can this be, since I do not know a man?" And the angel answered and said to her, "The Holy Spirit will come upon you, and the power of the Highest will overshadow you; therefore, also, that Holy One who is to be born will be called the Son of God. Now indeed, Elizabeth your relative has also conceived a son in her old age; and this is now the sixth month for her who was called barren. For with God nothing will be impossible." Then Mary said, "Behold the maidservant of the Lord! Let it be to me according to your word." And the angel departed from her (vv. 31-38).*

Unmarried and pregnant with a child of the Holy Ghost, faith never allowed her to dwell on the fact that she could be stoned or that Joseph would leave her or put her away privately—for becoming pregnant out of wedlock. She was able to rise above the humiliation and shame that society would try to put on her and accept her circumstances as a blessing—because she had a God-given priority of obedience and submission to the will of God. "Let it be to me according to your word" was her response to the angel Gabriel. Then, immediately after Mary received the news of her miraculous conception, we read in verse thirty-nine that she "… arose in those days and went into the hill country with haste, to a city of Judah." She entered into the house of Zacharias to be a blessing to Elizabeth, who—at that time—was six months pregnant with John the Baptist.

Mary understood the eternal significance of their pregnancies and could empathize with Elizabeth. Two expectant mothers, two unconventional pregnancies: one miraculous, the other outside the norm; both mothers were due to bare sons that would be more than just hated, but despised. Yet both sons would lead a multitude of people to God.

Mary's response at that time didn't just impact the "then and there"; it influenced the "here and now" as she faithfully served God by serving others. She balanced her priorities by making them God-centered as opposed to self-centered. As a result, she was sensitive to the prompting of the Holy Spirit, which led her to be a blessing to Elizabeth and all generations to come.

"And it happened, when Elizabeth heard the greeting of Mary, that the babe leaped in her womb; and Elizabeth was filled with the Holy Spirit. Then she spoke out with a loud voice and said, 'Blessed are you among women, and blessed is the fruit of your womb!'" (vv. 41-42).

Are you sensitive to the prompting of the Holy Spirit? Romans 8:14 reminds us that those who are guided by the Holy Spirit are God's children; and *blessed are you among women.*

Prayer

Lord, I humbly come before You, thanking You for giving Your only begotten Son that I might have life and have life more abundantly (John 10:10). Forgive me [for my sin of . . .]; and forgive me for allowing my circumstances to become a stumbling block in developing and maintaining an intimate relationship with You. I need Your help, Lord, to acquire balance and order in my daily life. Increase my effectiveness in Your kingdom by helping me to be led by Your Spirit. Open my mind's eyes, and allow me to see areas where You are calling me to have God-focused priorities. Fill me with Your love, and give me the strength, fortitude, focus, and wisdom to take the necessary steps to obtain balance and order—by making my priorities God-centered and not self-centered. I want all that I do to bring praise and glory to You. Thank You for Your grace and mercy. You are my strength, Lord. "Praise be to [Your] glorious name forever; may the whole earth be filled with [Your] glory" (Psalm 72:19, paraphrased). Amen.

- PONDER ON -

1. What does it mean to you to live a surrendered life?
....
....
....
....
....
....
....

2. What evidence in your life suggests that the spirit of God is leading you?
....
....
....
....
....
....
....

3. What changes in your life can you make so like Mary, you are more available to be used by God?
....
....
....
....
....
....

- NOTES -

> Whoever wants to be my disciple must deny themselves and take up their cross daily and follow me. ~ Luke 9:23

Step 2

Establishing Proper Priorities

Walk Worthy

PEOPLE AND THINGS, IF YOU ARE NOT WARY, WILL SEND YOU ON A DETOUR FROM THE PATH THAT GOD HAS FOR YOU. THE OPPORTUNITY TO BE A BLESSING AND TO BE BLESSED BY GOD IS IN YOUR OBEDIENCE TO HIS WORD AND IN YOUR ABILITY (WITH THE HOLY SPIRIT) TO STAY FOCUSED ON DOING HIS WILL.

STEP 2

From the Heart of God's Woman

Mary and Martha

Read: Luke 10:38-42

Mary, in the tenth chapter of Luke, is a pleasant reminder to us of choosing to be in the presence of God versus trying to appease someone else.

Can you imagine being a fly on the wall in the home of Martha and Mary? Every once in a while, Mary would take her eyes off of Jesus, only to lock eyes with her sister Martha, who was staring bitterly at her. With one hand, Martha's fingers were probably motioning "come here" while the other hand sat firmly on her hip. Martha was busy preparing food for her guests, while Mary—like a diligent student— sat at the feet of Jesus, listening to His words.

I imagine Mary wanted to be of service to Martha, who had always been there for her. They were probably close, so close they could almost guess what the other one was thinking, and at that moment, Martha's thoughts toward Mary were not pleasant.

Surely, Mary could not choose grinding grain, baking bread, setting the table, and washing dirty pots and pans over listening to the words that flowed from Jesus' mouth. Yes, these things needed to be done, but surely, they could wait. Jesus' words gave her peace that surpassed understanding, and His presence brought her comfort. There was no comparison.

Now it happened as they went that He (Jesus) entered a certain village; and a certain woman named Martha welcomed Him into her house. And she had a sister called Mary, who also sat at Jesus' feet and heard His word. But Martha was distracted with much serving, and she approached Him and said, "Lord, do You not care that my sister has left me to serve alone? Therefore tell her to help me." And Jesus answered and said to her, "Martha, Martha, you are worried and troubled about many things. But one thing is needed, and Mary has chosen that good part, which will not be taken away from her"(Luke 10:38-42).

There was no chastisement from Jesus over Martha's decision to serve; neither was Jesus going to judge Mary over her decision to sit in His presence. However, our Wonderful Counselor did prioritize what should be a primary priority for all Christians. He let us know *that one thing that was needed*, and that was love. The time Mary spent in the presence of Jesus was her heartfelt expression of her love for Him. Love prompted Mary to want to spend time with Jesus Christ.

One might argue that Martha loved Jesus just as much, but she allowed the cares of this world to hamper that love.

Like Martha, have you ever been so busy with the demands of daily life that you missed a day of spending time with God and in His Word? Then that one day turns into two days and two days into three days, and before you know it, you're not praying like you used to, and you've missed a couple of Sunday services. Maybe it's not busyness that has hindered your fellowship; perhaps you are depressed over circumstances in your life; maybe you're dealing with an illness or the illness of a loved one; perhaps you've suffered a great loss. Whatever may be hindering your fellowship with God, know that there is nothing greater than spending time in His presence.

Time in God's presence helped Mary discover what Martha had not yet realized: sacrificing time and attention doesn't always come easy. It requires a heightened state of awareness and understanding. A condition of mindfulness that immerses us in what matters most in the present moment. Every single day, we consciously choose to either allocate time to sit in the presence of God and the comfort of the Holy Spirit or to be consumed with housework, schoolwork, a spouse, a job, children, or other responsibilities.

Time belongs to God. The sacrifices we make to spend with God each day are rewarded with more time, more wisdom, more willpower, more patience, or more of a desire to be like Jesus Christ. God is no respect of persons; the same peace and contentment he gave Mary, He can provide to you.

Whenever you feel there is not enough time in your day, "Set your mind on things above, not on earthly things" (Colossians 3:2), and take heart in knowing that "…God is love. Whoever lives in love lives in God, and God in them." (1 John 4:16). Find balance in your service by committing your works unto God and cultivating awareness. When you make decisions from a place of mindfulness, you are less likely to act or react impulsively or be guided by your emotions.

Prayer

Lord, "Show me Your ways, O'Lord . . ." (Psalm 25:4). Help me to begin my day well. Let the thought of pleasing you be the first thing on my heart and mind when I wake up each morning. Reveal what can be eliminated from my day to help me focus on those things that are good and acceptable and bring glory to Your name. As I journey through this season of change, help me identify responsibilities and tasks that need my attention and due diligence. Open my eyes to hindrances within myself or around me that keep me from spending quality time each day in Your presence: praying, praising, reading Your Word, and meditating on Your goodness. Please help me find the right balance between family, work, and other activities. Enable me to operate in a state of mindfulness. Lord, You know my ways; when You have tested me, let me come forth as gold (Job 23:10). Thank You, Lord, for I know You are a good God, Your mercy and love are everlasting, and Your "truth endures to all generations" (Psalm 100:5). Amen.

STEP 2

- PONDER ON -

1. What significance does Jesus' death on the cross have on your daily priorities?

....
....
....
....
....
....

2. Have you ever been in a situation where you neglected to put God first? What did it cost you (time, money, embarrassment, etc.)?

....
....
....
....
....
....

3. List some things you do daily; then comb through your list. Are you doing those things out of love or duty?

....
....
....
....
....
....

- NOTES -

> But seek first his kingdom and his righteousness, and all these things will be given to you as well. ~ Matt. 6:33

Step 3

Prayerfully Planning Ahead

There is absolutely nothing we can do about the unexpected but expect it. Lack of direction, lack of commitment, and wrong motivation are surface excuses rooted in the spirit of distrust. Failing to trust God to give us divine direction, to order our steps... then giving us the fortitude and resilience to stay committed to the course.

STEP 3

From the Heart of God's Woman

Esther

Read: Esther 3:1-7:10

Esther paces the floor, wringing her hands together, nervous about Mordecai's public display of concern. He was at the palace in front of the king's gate, dressed in sackcloth and ashes and very distressed over a recent decree that had been distributed throughout the Persian Empire.

After her parents had died, her older relative Mordecai raised her as his daughter and insisted that she compete with thousands of other women for the title of Queen. Despite the odds and her apprehensions, she had won the affection of King Ahasuerus and was chosen to replace his wife Vashti—who was dethroned after refusing to come at his bidding.

After having lived a relatively meager but pleasant life with Mordecai, her life had turned out pretty good; filled with servants, material possessions, social opportunities, and whatever she desired—with few restrictions. So, it was understandable that she did not know how to receive the message she had just been given from Mordecai. The lives of her people were in danger. According to the decree, non-Jews were given permission "... to destroy, to kill, and to annihilate all the Jews, both young and old, little children and women, in one day, on the thirteenth day of twelfth month, which is the month of Adar, and to plunder their possessions" (Esther 3:13). Her heart sank as she realized the decree was signed and approved by her husband, King Ahasuerus.

Apprehension set in as she was confronted with her options. If she attempted to go before her husband to intercede for her people without being called, she would be jeopardizing her own life. She let Mordecai know that; in return, Mordecai let her know that she would not be exempt from the wrath of Haman, the King's Prime Minister, whose evil mind drafted the decree. Mordecai's message to Queen Esther was:

> "Do not think in your heart that you will escape in the king's palace any more than all the other Jews. For if you remain completely silent at this time, relief and deliverance will arise for the Jews from another place, but you and your father's house will perish. Yet who knows whether you have come to the kingdom for such a time as this?" (4:13-14).

His words pierced her heart, and she immediately goes into a period of prayerful planning. She sends word to Mordecai to tell all the Jews in Shushan to: "... fast for me; neither eat nor drink for three days, night or day. My maids and I will fast likewise. And so I will go to the king, which is against the law; and if I perish, I perish!" (v. 16).

After three days of fasting, she gains the courage to go uninvited before the king, and he receives her by holding out the golden scepter. She invites the king and Haman to her banquet but does not reveal her desires—she is still in the midst of prayerful planning. Then, she asks the king and Haman to join her on a second day for yet another banquet. After the second banquet and after prayerful planning, when she found peace in her heart that God's will shall be done, she disclosed her desire to the king, who responded with love and compassion.

Life can seem so wonderful at times until the unexpected happens, and we are jarred into reality, exiled from our own comfort and contentment, and forced to take a new direction, to step into a strange territory, or to jump in the midst of something we never experienced before. That unexpected thing thrust upon us could be losing a job, getting a divorce, having our life threatened, or losing a loved one. The options are endless, but one thing is for sure: your life will never be the same, and like Esther, you are where you are right now for such a time as this; ask God to show you what it is.

Having an awareness of the need for God is essential in prayerful planning. Although God knows your circumstances, He wants you to come to Him. Prayerful planning is praying for God's guidance and direction in any given situation. Whatever guidance is given, you receive it in faith, and you act on the wisdom provided by God. Hebrews 11:6 reminds us: "But without faith it is impossible to please Him, for he who comes to God must believe that He is, and that He is a rewarder of those who diligently seek Him."

When it comes to planning, prayerful consideration is crucial. This involves identifying priorities and coordinating with God to determine which goals and objectives should take precedence—so your time, energy, and resources are appropriately balanced. If unforeseen circumstances arise, you can make the necessary adjustments because your heart and mind are attuned to God.

Prayer

Most gracious God, help me improve the quality of my day by praying about my day and planning my day wisely. Bless my efforts to prayerfully plan. Please guide me in assuming responsibility for how my day is being spent. I realize that unexpected events can and will occur. When I sit down to establish goals or to write out a task list, I want to be attuned to Your will—even if it means setting aside my goals and tasks for the day to be used by you to bless others. Help me to order my days so that they bring honor and glory to You. Place within me the desire to read and study Your Word and be recharged by it. Bless me each day to complete the necessary tasks before me by breaking tasks down into specific, actionable, and achievable steps. Most importantly, keep me mindful that anything I do that is of eternal value requires dependence upon You. Thank You, Lord, for doing "...exceedingly abundantly above all that [I] ask or think, according to the power that works in [me]" (Ephesians 3:20, emphasis added). Amen.

- PONDER ON -

1. How would you define "prayerful planning"?
....
....
....
....
....
....

2. Have you ever been confronted with a major decision that impacted a life or lives? How did you respond (e.g., was your initial instinct to go into a period of prayerful planning or seeking spiritual guidance)?
....
....
....
....
....
....

3. What are some things God has been nudging you to do more often? Pray, and ask God to show you how to fit those things into your day.
....
....
....
....
....

- NOTES -

Trust in the Lord with all your heart and lean not on your own understanding;

~ Prov. 3:5

Step 4

Exercising and Eating Healthy

dance and rejoice

TO GLORIFY GOD WITH YOUR BODY MEANS YOU GIVE GOD THE FIRST FRUIT OF YOUR WORSHIP AND THE BEST OF YOUR SERVICE. THE ONLY WAY TO EFFECTIVELY DO THAT IS TO TAKE CARE OF THE BODY HE HAS BLESSED YOU WITH—SO THAT YOU ARE MENTALLY AND SPIRITUALLY WELL ENOUGH AND PHYSICALLY ABLE TO CARRY OUT HIS WILL HERE ON EARTH.

STEP 4

From the Heart of God's Woman

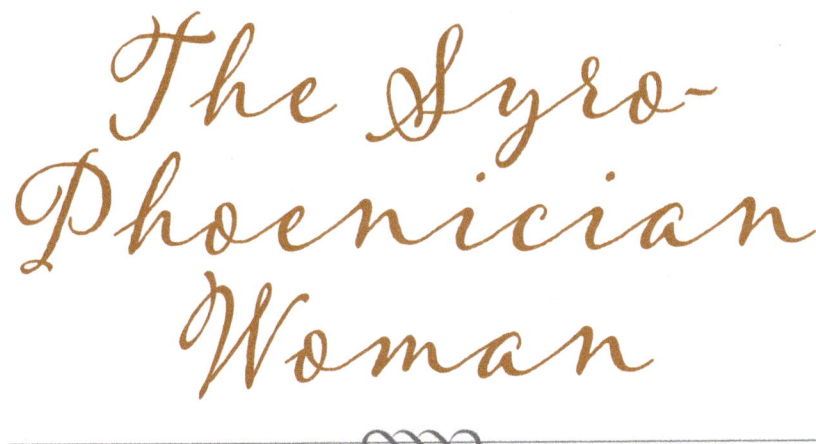
The Syro-Phoenician Woman

Read: Matthew 15:21-28

The Syro-Phoenician woman was residing in the region of Tyre and Sidon, when she sought Jesus for her daughter's healing. Let us go back through the passageway of time as we step into the shoes, heart, and mind of the Syro-Phoenician mother, desperately seeking healing for her child.

She closed the door behind her, leaving her daughter inside with relatives. Taking in a deep breath, she briskly sets out on her journey, eagerly wanting each step forward to bring her closer to Jesus. She had heard that Jesus was nearby, and although not of Jewish descent, she would seek Him for her daughter's healing, anyway.

Family, friends, and neighbors had been talking about a man who was unlike any other. "[He] went about all the cities and villages, teaching in their synagogues, preaching the gospel of the kingdom, and healing every sickness and every disease among the people" (Matthew 9:35, emphasis added). There were even talks that He had healed a demon-possessed man and made a leper clean by His touch.

As she walked and prayed silently, faith had her believing that Jesus was the one. He was the Messiah who would bring healing to her daughter.

As she approached a slow-moving crowd, she immediately wondered if she had found the Messiah. Her heart was pounding feverishly as she attempted to push her way through the crowd, but it was as if people were finely woven together, deliberately trying to keep her from Jesus.

Finally, like piercing through a keyhole in a door, she gets a glimpse of Him. "Have mercy on me, O Lord, Son of David! My daughter is severely demon-possessed" (Matthew 15:22), she cried out, forcing a break in the crowd as people turned to stare at her. Paying them no mind, she persisted forward. She was there for a purpose; if she needed to grovel and beg, she would gladly humble herself before Jesus so that her daughter might be healed.

While pressing past the people, Jesus' disciples tried to deter her, to no avail. So they turned to Jesus and said, "Send her away, for she cries out after us" (v. 23). Jesus turns towards her with a sigh of impatience, then addresses her by saying, "I was not sent except to the lost sheep of the house of Israel" (v. 24). After hearing His response, she falls on her knees out of worship, respect, and pure exhaustion. Jesus was her last hope; she could bear this cross no more. With her tear-stained face and through strained breath, she softly mutters the words: "Lord, help me!" (v. 25). Sensing her desperation, what might have been perceived as a slight earlier now turns into sympathy. He engages in a dialogue with her:

He answered and said, "It is not good to take the children's bread and throw it to the little dogs." And she said, "Yes, Lord, yet even the little dogs eat the crumbs which fall from their masters' table." Then Jesus answered and said to her, "O woman, great is your faith! Let it be to you as you desire." And her daughter was healed from that very hour (vv. 26-28).

I once heard a pastor give a sermon entitled: "How Big Is Your God?" The question gets to the heart of how much faith and trust do you have in God, that if you have a need, He is able and willing to provide or work out an impossible circumstance on your behalf.

How big is your God? That question brings to mind how so many people are limiting God from doing the impossible. Jesus had come to the lost sheep of the house of Israel, but that did not hinder the Syro-Phoenician woman from seeking what God could provide.

Through the Syro-Phoenician woman, we see a woman whose prevailing persistence paid off, mowing down hindrances to bring her to what she desired most—healing for her daughter. We also see a woman who prepared her heart before going before God. How else could she respond to Jesus' question with such faith? Finally, she placed herself in the pathway to be blessed.

Mark 7:30 says, "When she had come to her house, she found the demon gone, and her daughter lying on the bed."

Do you need healing? *Balance* begs for an answer to the question: How big is your God? Are you accepting the crumbs that have fallen to the ground when a big feast is on the table before you?

Prayer

Father, as I continue to balance my blessings, help me pray with a higher level of expectation—place within my heart the faith and boldness of the Syro-Phoenician woman. "Grant Your strength to Your servant" (Psalm 86:16). When I encounter difficulty on the road to establishing a healthy lifestyle or getting healing, remind me to turn to You for guidance. Help me release unhealthy habits and negative behavior that may affect my health, my fellowship with You, and my relationship with others. Reveal hindrances keeping me from receiving the blessings You wish to bestow upon me. May Your glory fill me when I feel stressed and depressed and want to [e.g., give up...]. Touch me, Lord. Let Your healing hand be on me, my loved loves, and all those in need. Cover me, Lord. Let Your hedge of protection keep me and my loved ones safe and secure within Your everlasting arms. Thank You for all Your glorious creations, and "[I] know that all things work together for good to those who love God, to those who are the called according to [Your] purpose" (Romans 8:28, emphasis added). Amen.

- PONDER ON -

1. If you desperately needed God's healing for yourself or a loved one, how would you approach the throne of God? Would you come expecting crumbs when a big feast is before you?

....
....
....
....
....

2. Write what you feel drives you to engage in self-destructive habits (e.g., smoking when you feel anxious or eating when you feel stressed). Decide whether to seek counseling.

....
....
....
....
....

3. How do you feel about your present health? What actions are you committed to taking that will improve your overall health?

....
....
....
....
....

- NOTES -

> For you were bought at a price; therefore glorify God in your body and in your spirit, which are God's. ~ 1 Cor. 6:20

Step 5

Conquering Your Clutter

How insignificant our clutter may seem to us versus preaching God's word and ministering to the masses, but if we are to obey God, should we not obey God in all things? Our minds, hearts, and souls yearn for order. A desire put there by our Creator. This is evident in the fact that our effectiveness for God increases when there is order in our daily lives.

STEP 5

From the Heart of God's Woman

The Woman with the Alabaster Box

Read: Luke 7:36-50

She was *the woman with the alabaster box*—considered a notorious harlot with many sins. She was also an uninvited guest in the house of Simon the Leper, a Pharisee. Upon entering, she could hear the snickering of the men and feel their stares of judgment as she quickly and quietly walked to where Jesus was reclining and humbly knelt down at His feet.

Holding her alabaster box of fine perfume, her mind and heart were galloping with emotions of fear, joy, and love. She had heard Jesus speak before and could not shake the words—that resonated from His heart to her heart—from her soul. Entrenched so deeply in her sin, it was His grace that gave her the courage to get out of her sin and then led her to a place where she was not welcomed but would feel welcomed in the presence of Jesus.

Besieged by God's grace, she began to "wash the feet of Jesus with her tears," not considering that the tears streaming from her eyes were settling on feet that would soon be pierced for her transgressions.

Anointing Him with her precious perfume and wiping His feet with her hair was the only way to demonstrate her heartfelt love to a man who had first loved her, had forgiven her of all her sins, and had ministered to her wounded soul with compassion. Luke 7:37-39 captures for us that moment in time:

> *And behold, a woman in the city who was a sinner, when she knew that Jesus sat at the table in the Pharisee's house, brought an alabaster flask of fragrant oil, and stood at His feet behind Him weeping; and she began to wash His feet with her tears, and wiped them with the hair of her head; and she kissed His feet and anointed them with the fragrant oil. Now when the Pharisee who had invited Him saw this, he spoke to himself, saying, "This Man, if He were a prophet, would know who and what manner of woman this is who is touching Him, for she is a sinner."*

This woman's guilt and self-condemnation over her past iniquities preceded her. It followed her everywhere she went; it was what most people noticed first about her, including the assembly of men in Simon's house.

Have you ever walked into a place where you knew you needed to be but felt like you were a stranger, an outcast, an oddball, or an uninvited guest? Maybe this place is school, church, work, or perhaps home carries a stigma. Every time someone sees you there, they also see your pain, circumstances, notorious reputation, or what you did to them. You're the one who committed that lewd act, had a drunken fit, a cheating husband, or was the victim of someone's imprudence. You long for people to forget, let it go, or get amnesia—so you can be who Jesus Christ created you to be. "That was yesterday," you want to cry out, "Today, I've been forgiven, and I have forgiven!"

Jesus, in His omniscience, understood the emotions driving this woman's actions. Capable of diving into the thoughts of others, He also knew the thoughts swirling in Simon's mind regarding this woman. Like a protective father defending the honor of his daughter, one can only picture Jesus rising from his reclining position enough to look Simon squarely in the eyes and into his heart. He says to Simon in Luke 7:44-47:

> *"Do you see this woman? I entered your house; you gave Me no water for My feet, but she has washed My feet with her tears and wiped them with the hair of her head. You gave Me no kiss, but this woman has not ceased to kiss My feet since the time I came in. You did not anoint My head with oil, but this woman has anointed My feet with fragrant oil. Therefore I say to you, her sins, which are many, are forgiven, for she loved much. But to whom little is forgiven, the same loves little."*

Then Jesus immediately turned to address the woman with four simple but powerful words: "Your sins are forgiven."

That's the beauty of God's love; His love sees our worth when others don't. He offers us what no man has ever been able to give: a love that transcends man's understanding, a love that heals and forgives, a love that sacrificed His son for our iniquities. Receiving and accepting God's love is a transformative experience, bringing with it a profound sense of purpose, community, and a peaceful state of mind that goes beyond the highs and lows of what others think about us.

Prayer

Lord, I am grateful for your generosity and the many blessings you have bestowed upon me. Continue to open my heart and mind; show me how You want me to live my life. Infuse me with Your wisdom to distinguish between my desires and Your desires for me. Help me put more worth and value in obtaining knowledge from Your Word than worldly possessions, pursuits, or pleasures. Lord, I invite You into my domain; help me to conquer the clutter in my home and any sin in my life. Reveal to me what items in my home can be given to bless someone else and to glorify You. Let me not covet the blessings You have bestowed on others, but let my mind be content with the sacrifices You have made for many. As Your Word eloquently states in 1 Timothy 6:6: "…godliness with contentment is great gain." Thank You for helping me bring order to my chaos so that I might be a greater blessing to others. Thank You for cleansing me with Your blood, "clothing me with the garments of salvation, and covering me with the robe of righteousness" (Isaiah 61:10, paraphrased). Amen. ❧

- PONDER ON -

1. Have you ever visited a place where God called you to be, but felt like an uninvited guest? Describe how you felt.

....
....
....
....
....

2. Have you ever felt wrongly judged and ostracized by family and friends? How did that make you feel?

....
....
....
....
....
....

3. Reflect on Isaiah 61:10. How does it feel to be clothed with garments of salvation and arrayed in a robe of His righteousness?

....
....
....
....
....
....

- NOTES -

Do not store up for yourselves treasures on earth, where moths and vermin destroy, and where thieves break in and steal. ~ Matt. 6:19

Step 6

Evolving through Productive Pursuits

LIFE WILL HAVE ITS CHALLENGES. THERE WILL BE MOMENTS WHEN YOU WILL FEEL UTTERLY DESERTED, CONFUSED ABOUT THE TWISTS AND TURNS YOUR LIFE HAS TAKEN TO BRING YOU TO YOUR PRESENT CIRCUMSTANCES. SOMETIMES, YOUR CIRCUMSTANCES ARE TO HELP YOU EXPERIENCE THE FULLNESS AND DEPTH OF GOD'S LOVE IN A DIFFERENT LIGHT OF UNDERSTANDING. SOMETIMES, CIRCUMSTANCES EXIST SO THAT YOU MAY BE THE SALT AND LIGHT FOR OTHERS.

STEP 6

From the Heart of God's Woman

Read: Judges 4:1-5:9

Deborah is an exemplary example of the multifaceted woman talked about in Proverbs 31. Though nothing is provided to give us a complete picture of how she looked, we do get an extraordinary portrait of who she was.

If we review her profile, we see her strengths were serving, caring, preaching, praying, and counseling. Her passion was seeing that the commands of God and His desires for His people were carried out, as she used her gifts to minister and aid the people of Israel.

Day by day, one by one, the children of Israel came from Ramah and Bethel so that Deborah could judge their matters in her courthouse, under a palm tree, in the mountains of Ephraim. She worked in a male-dominated environment, but we never read about her stepping over people demanding her rights; neither did she sit passively on the sidelines.

She understood her spiritual calling by using her spiritual gifts to prophesy over and edify Israel. She also understood her natural calling as the wife of Lappidoth, a mother, and a judge over the people of Israel.

People were drawn to her godly wisdom, inner beauty, and strength. When she prophesied, it came to pass, which was why she was highly regarded not just by women but also by men, including General Barak.

After twenty years of oppression under King Jabin of Hazor, a Canaanite king, Israel cried out to God. God heard their pleas, created a vision for their deliverance, and passed that vision on to Deborah in the form of a prophetic message.

> *Then she sent and called for Barak the son of Abinoam from Kedesh in Naphtali, and said to him, "Has not the LORD God of Israel commanded, 'Go and deploy troops at Mount Tabor; take with you ten thousand men ... and against you I will deploy Sisera, the commander of Jabin's army, with his chariots and his multitude at the River Kishon; and I will deliver him into your hand'?" And Barak said to her, "If you will go with me, then I will go; but if you will not go with me, I will not go!" So she said, "I will surely go with you; nevertheless there will be no glory for you in the journey you are taking, for the LORD will sell Sisera into the hand of a woman." Then Deborah arose and went with Barak to Kedesh (Judges 4:6-9).*

Anyone can certainly empathize with General Barak's reluctance to go alone on a mission God called him to accomplish. It's much more pleasant having a friend or mate by our side for morale support—that's understandable. But what God is looking for is courageous people, men and women willing to step out of the boat like Peter, regardless of whether someone comes with them, and trust Him to provide everything they need to accomplish the mission He has placed in their hearts to do.

Step 6

Deborah complied with the General's request to accompany him to Kedesh. She wasn't distrait with thoughts about what the Jabin's garrison commander would do. Her thoughts were firmly on the victory the Lord promised: *to deliver Sisera into Israel's hands.*

When Sisera got wind that Barak had gone up to Mount Tabor with his men, he gathered together all his chariots—determined to crush any uprising. With nine hundred iron chariots and all his troops, Sisera pursued Barak from Harosheth Hagoyim to the Kishon River (v. 13).

> *Then Deborah said to Barak, "Up! For this is the day in which the Lord has delivered Sisera into your hand.... So Barak went down from Mount Tabor with ten thousand men following him. And the Lord routed Sisera and all his chariots and all his army with the edge of the sword before Barak; and Sisera alighted from his chariot and fled away on foot. But Barak pursued the chariots and the army as far as Harosheth Hagoyim, and all the army of Sisera fell by the edge of the sword; not a man was left (Judges 4:14-16).*

Deborah's obedience, predicated on faith, put her in a leadership role when a patriarchal culture would have forbidden it. Her obedience was contagious. It spread to General Barak and throughout Israel in the form of influence. As a result, King Jabin and his kingdom were destroyed. Coincidentally, upon their victory, Deborah and Barak savor the movement in praise and worship with a song to inspire the people that begins with: "When leaders lead in Israel...."

Do you see yourself as a leader? Judges 5:7 tells us that Deborah considered herself "a mother in Israel." What a humble response from God's leading lady, who played a leading role in leading a multitude of men into battle.

Prayer

Heavenly Father, please grant me Your divine wisdom as I pursue productive endeavors. I pray that Your wisdom will enable me to make the right decisions, choose the right paths, and take the right actions that will lead me to bring glory and honor to Your name. Aid me in binding those things in my life [e.g., fear, depression, low self-esteem, sickness, etc.] that are hindering me from serving you effectively. Manifest the fruit of the Spirit in my life, and give me the energy, wisdom, direction, and courage to discover and pursue the passions You have placed in my heart. Make my motives right before you. I want to be the salt and light for others. Fill me up when I am thirsty: thirsty for love, thirsty for acceptance, or thirsty for acknowledgment. Make me like a "watered garden, like a spring of water, whose water never fail" (Isaiah 58:11). Most Wonderful Counselor, as you position me to minister to others, filter my words through Your Word. "Let the words of my mouth and the meditation of my heart Be acceptable in Your sight, O Lord, my strength and my Redeemer" (Psalm 19:14). Amen.

- PONDER ON -

1. What characteristics, in your opinion, assess whether a person exhibits the qualities and behaviors associated with an effective leader?

....
....
....
....
....

2. Do you see yourself as a leader (i.e., are you the *salt and light* for others, can you inspire and motivate others to follow your lead)?

....
....
....
....
....
....

3. What three steps can you take to prepare yourself for a leadership role, promotion, or to develop those qualities you admire in others?

....
....
....
....
....

- NOTES -

> "I am the vine; you are the branches. If you remain in me and I in you, you will bear much fruit; apart from me you can do nothing." ~ John 15:5

Step 7

Reviving Your Relationships

RELATIONSHIPS TAKE HARD WORK AND COMMITMENT; RUNNING AWAY AND ISOLATING YOURSELF DOES NOT ELIMINATE THE FACT THAT YOU WERE DESIGNED TO HAVE RELATIONSHIPS, WHICH IS MORE THAN JUST BEING IN THE MIDST OF PEOPLE. IT'S INTERACTING AND CONNECTING WITH PEOPLE ON A PERSONAL LEVEL. THIS INCLUDES COMPANIONSHIP AND FELLOWSHIP BUT GOES BEYOND THE TWO TO THE CORE OF RELATIONSHIPS: TO GLORIFY GOD.

STEP 6

From the Heart of God's Woman

Abigail

Read: I Samuel 25:2-42

Abigail is introduced in 1 Samuel 25:3 as a woman "of good understanding and beautiful." She was a classic example of Webster's definition of a gracious woman: kind and courteous. Yet, Abigail was married to a foolish man named Nabal. Christians have dubbed them as the beauty and the beast of the Old Testament. A god-fearing, tender-hearted, and generous woman bonded together in holy matrimony with the abuser, the drunkard, the player, or the master manipulator.

If we were to sit down to listen to Abigail's story, she would probably share how charming he was when they dated. He impressed her with his humorous banter and generous nature—bringing Frankincense for her mother, wine for her father, and assorted fruits for her siblings. He was passionate about building a stable and fertile life for his family. He had been genuine in her eyes, only for those genuine gestures to wear away with time.

There were early signs, but she didn't want to see them; because of her strong desire to love and be loved, she learned to adjust to him—faults and all—regardless of how his behavior affected her.

If she had listened to her friends and not God, she'd been gone. They could never understand how the truth of God's loving wisdom could help her understand her man for who he was and is. Whether it's the little boy who wasn't raised with a father around who doesn't appreciate that marriage is a partnership, not a dictatorship. Or whether it's the young man who learned to survive the streets by outwitting people, currently manipulates his wife, boss, friends, and coworkers. Despite his issues, she gets him and loves him, regardless.

However, no matter how much Abigail loved Nabal, she still had boundaries—especially when lives were in danger.

We are told in I Samuel 25 that after days of voluntarily protecting Nabal's livestock in the wilderness, David sought favor from Nabal, a very wealthy man with 3,000 sheep and 1,000 goats. Nabal was shearing sheep in Carmel when David sent ten men to greet him and request a generous offering of food and other sustenance. David and his army had protected Nabal's sheep, goats, and shepherds from danger. Nabal's servant described them as a "wall to us both by night and day." In exchange, David asked for charity so his men would have food on the *feast day*. Nabal's response was heartless. Instead of showing gratitude for what the men had done, he reviled them. So, when the men returned and shared what was said, David responded with a burst of anger over Nabal's callous words. He told about four hundred men to "gird on [your] swords."

A discerning servant, perceiving the harm that might come to his master's household, informed Abigail of the situation. Abigail quickly mustered up enough sustenance to feed a small

STEP 6

army. She then flung herself onto a donkey to intercede on her husband's behalf. Now, when Abigail saw David:

> ... she fell at his feet and said: "On me, my lord, on me let this iniquity be! And please let your maidservant speak in your ears, and hear the words of your maidservant. Please, let not my lord regard this scoundrel Nabal.... But I, your maidservant, did not see the young men of my lord whom you sent. Now therefore, ... since the Lord has held you back from coming to bloodshed and from avenging yourself with your own hand, now then, let your enemies and those who seek harm for my lord be as Nabal. And now this present which your maidservant has brought to my lord, let it be given to the young men who follow my lord. Please forgive the trespass of your maidservant. For the Lord will certainly make for my lord an enduring house, because my lord fights the battles of the Lord, and evil is not found in you throughout your days. And it shall come to pass, when the Lord has done for my lord according to all the good that He has spoken concerning you, and has appointed you ruler over Israel, ... then remember your maidservant" (I Samuel 25:24-28, 31).

Like Abigail, sometimes you must realize when a relationship jeopardizes lives. Then, you must take a stand, if not for yourself, for those who cannot stand for themselves. When Abigail left to greet David, it was to quell his anger and save her household.

Abigail's story provides a beautiful example of a woman who welcomed wisdom to help her find balance in her relationship with her husband. She also did not hesitate to act upon wisdom's call to do what needed to be done or to say what needed to be said. Abigail was able to act out of wisdom and speak the truth in love because her heart was in the right place.

Prayer

"O Lord, our Lord, How excellent is Your name in all the earth, Who have set Your glory above the heavens!" (Psalm 8:1). Lord, transform my heart and give me a renewed perspective on my relationships so I can make the necessary adjustments to rekindle my relationship with those You have reopened my heart to. I want to be a reflection of Your unwavering love. Strengthen my heart and grant me the ability to shower them with the same love and compassion you have shown me. When I speak, let it be with clarity of thought so that I am understood; with wisdom, that my words inspire, heal, and encourage; and with discernment, so that I know when to speak and when to be silent. When family members, friends, associates, or coworkers are going through a difficult circumstance, let my words be a source of inspiration that lifts their spirits. Thank You, Lord, for transforming me from glory to glory (2 Corinthians 3:18) and teaching me how to be kind-hearted, compassionate, and forgiving toward others, just as You forgave me (Ephesians 4:32). Amen.

STEP 6

- PONDER ON -

1. People's emotional energy stemming from past experiences can affect us whether we realize it. What steps can you take to establish healthy boundaries or to help make your encounter with them bearable?

....
....
....
....
....

2. How do you handle situations where a loved one fails to keep their commitments or their behavior changes in a way that contradicts your values?

....
....
....
....
....
....

3. What steps can you take to help mend a broken relationship between yourself and a difficult family member?

....
....
....
....
....

- NOTES -

> Blessed are the peacemakers,
> for they will be called children of God.
>
> ~ Matt. 5:9

Step 8

Making Your Ministry Matter

be transformed

YOUR LIFE AND MINISTRY MATTERS TO GOD! THE BITTER DIVORCE THAT LEFT YOU DESTITUTE, BROKE, OR DEPRESSED, MATTERS. THE DEATH OF YOUR LOVED ONE THAT CAUSED YOUR WORLD TO CRUMBLE, MATTERS. THE ABILITY TO MOVE PEOPLE WITH YOUR SONGSTRESS VOICE, MATTERS. THE SKILL TO SWAY A PERSON TO BUY A PRODUCT YOU'RE SELLING, MATTERS. ANY TIME YOU ALLOW GOD TO USE YOU TO BLESS OTHERS, YOU'RE MINISTERING.

STEP 8

From the Heart of God's Woman

Read: John 4:1-38

She was *the woman from Samaria*, an outcast to the Jews and a disgrace to her people because of her lifestyle. Yet, her ministry mattered and made a difference in the lives of others. Let us reflect on that crucial moment when she meets Jesus Christ, her Lord and Savior.

It was the sixth hour of the day; she clutched the handles of her water pots with one hand and, with the other, flung open the back door of her home to catch that inconspicuous trail leading to Jacob's well.

Since it was the hottest and most humid part of the day, few people would be at the well, but that was what she wanted. She had heard enough of the jokes, laughter, and whispers, and had received more than her share of raised eyebrows and stares of judgment from the men and women in the city. She longed to flee to a place where no one knew her and where no one would judge her for her past iniquities.

Beaten down with guilt, she could not dispute the fact that she had left her husbands, taken other women's husbands, and was still searching for a husband to fill the gnawing emptiness deep in the pit of her heart.

It was hot, she thought to herself before noticing a man reclining against the well. She went about her business; he was a Jew, and Jews have no dealings with Samaritans—even though Jewish blood flowed through her veins.

"... Give Me a drink" (John 4:7), she heard the man say; startled she said, "... How is it that You, being a Jew, ask a drink from me, a Samaritan woman?" (v. 9). Jesus responded by saying, "If you knew the gift of God, and who it is who says to you, 'Give Me a drink,' you would have asked Him, and He would have given you living water" (v. 10).

Her people only spoke to her when it was necessary or when they desired something, but here was a man with a gift for her. Her curiosity peaked as she said, "Sir, You have nothing to draw with, and the well is deep. Where then do You get that living water? Are You greater than our father Jacob, who gave us the well, and drank from it himself, as well as his sons and his livestock?" (vv. 11-12).

She was probing Him. She could see He had nothing to draw with—no skin, cup, or vessel to drink from. So she supposed that He was a great prophet. The dialogue continues:

> *Jesus answered and said to her, "Whoever drinks of this water will thirst again but whoever drinks of the water that I shall give him will never thirst. But the water that I shall give him will become in him a fountain of water springing up into everlasting life." The woman said to Him, "Sir, give me this water, that I may not thirst, nor come here to draw."*

Jesus said to her, "Go, call your husband, and come here." The woman answered and said, "I have no husband." Jesus said to her, "You have well said, 'I have no husband,' for you have had five husbands, and the one whom you now have is not your husband; in that you spoke truly." "But the hour is coming, and now is, when the true worshipers will worship the Father in spirit and truth; for the Father is seeking such to worship Him. God is Spirit, and those who worship Him must worship in spirit and truth." The woman said to Him, "I know that Messiah is coming" (who is called Christ). "When He comes, He will tell us all things." Jesus said to her, "I who speak to you am He" (John 4:13-18, 23-26).

That day at the well, Jesus gave this woman the gift of eternal life and a ministry that mattered.

Her heart had been broken many times, and her spirit had been humbled by her circumstances. It's no wonder that she eagerly desired the living water Jesus was offering. Her response to hearing the Gospel was to give what had been given to her. She left all that she had brought with her to the well (her water pots, her past, her pain, her guilt, her sins, etc.); she then went into the city and said to the men: "Come, see a Man who told me all things that I ever did. Could this be the Christ?"

In one day, in one brief moment in time, God had spread her wings, and like a beautiful butterfly, she took flight in the ministry God had equipped and empowered her to soar in. No longer would people see her and think of her sins; from that day forward, people would see her and then see Jesus Christ in her. All because she purposed in her heart to give what had been given to her, and in doing so, she led many to Jesus Christ.

Prayer

Precious Lord, reign in my heart. When my faith begins to fade, sustain me. Help me to walk in the power of the Holy Spirit instead of in my own power. Examine my heart and know my anxieties; test me and know my thoughts. See if there is any wicked way in me, and guide me on the path of eternal life (Psalm 139:23-24, paraphrased). May Your Spirit be my constant companion in leading me on the path of righteousness and keeping me steady on level ground. Inspire me to be more diligent in sharing the Gospel with others. Remove barriers that have hindered me in the past. When I feel prompted, reveal to me the most effective way to share the message of salvation with individuals who need to hear it. Let there be joy in my heart when I tell them that "[You] have come that they may have life, and that they may have it more abundantly" (John 10:10, emphasis added). Assist me in identifying and understanding my spiritual gifts, and give me the desire to use them to honor you and edify the Body of Christ. Thank You, Lord, for loving me and giving me the opportunity to serve. Amen.

- PONDER ON -

1. If Jesus were to meet you at the well, what attitude, behavior, or dark area of your life would He have to shine the light of His Spirit on for His truth to bring you to confession and repentance?

....
....
....
....
....

2. When was the last time you shared your faith with someone? How did it feel to introduce someone to Jesus Christ?

....
....
....
....
....
....

3. If you have never or rarely shared your faith, what barriers have prevented you from sharing your faith with others?

....
....
....
....
....

- NOTES -

...be transformed by the renewing of your mind, that you may prove what is that good, acceptable, and perfect will of God. ~ Rom. 12:2

Step 9

Getting Financially Focused

seek treasures above

BESIDES HAVING A FINANCIAL VISION AND SETTING FINANCIAL GOALS, I AM CONVINCED THAT ECONOMIC SUCCESS FOR ANY CHILD OF GOD BEGINS WITH PRAYER. IF THERE IS A DESIRE TO REVERSE YOUR FINANCIAL SITUATION, IT SHOULD COME WITH A DESIRE TO REPENT OR CHANGE YOUR ACTIONS AND THOUGHTS REGARDING YOUR MONEY AND POSSESSIONS.

STEP 9

From the Heart of God's Woman

———⊰⊱———

Read: 2 King 4:1-7

The Prophet's Widow. Have you ever found yourself in a situation where the person you loved with all your heart was no longer a part of your life? Whether God took them or they decided they no longer wanted to be with you, they were gone.

The Old Testament shares a story about a widow who had to bury her husband and then, without a chance to mourn, had to deal with the household finances. Let us turn the clock back and imagine, for a moment, what it might have been like for the widow described in 2 Kings 4:1-7.

There was a hard knock at the door that startled her. She quickly looks at her sons and motions for them to be silent. She didn't need to answer the door to know who it was or what he wanted. He was back, threatening to take her sons if he did not get his money.

She feared opening the door, having told the creditor repeatedly that she had nothing to give to pay her husband's debt. Everything in her house was gone. The only possession she owned was a jar of oil, and the only items of personal value to her were her sons—which she refused to give up. Devastated, broke, and destitute, she sought God's protection and provision for herself and her sons. Here is her story:

> *A certain woman of the wives of the sons of the prophets cried out to Elisha, saying, "Your servant my husband is dead, and you know that your servant feared the LORD. And the creditor is coming to take my two sons to be his slaves." So Elisha said to her, "What shall I do for you? Tell me, what do you have in the house?" And she said, "Your maidservant has nothing in the house but a jar of oil." Then he said, "Go, borrow vessels from everywhere, from all your neighbors—empty vessels; do not gather just a few. And when you have come in, you shall shut the door behind you and your sons; then pour it into all those vessels, and set aside the full ones." So she went from him and shut the door behind her and her sons.... Now it came to pass, when the vessels were full, that she said to her son, "Bring me another vessel." And he said to her, "There is not another vessel." So the oil ceased. Then she came and told the man of God. And he said, "Go, sell the oil and pay your debt; and you and your sons live on the rest"* (2 Kings 4:1-7).

Many women can relate to the struggles faced by this widow, as similar challenges persist in modern society. Despite the advancements made by women in the workplace, they are still likely to be devastated financially when a spouse leaves due to death or divorce without making proper provisions for their family. Similarly, financial hardship can affect anyone, regardless of their background, when they experience job loss, medical bills, inflation, natural disasters, or other life events.

Anyone can fall victim to exploitation due to financial vulnerability, regardless of their race, gender, or nationality. However, our most gracious God can meet you where you are. He can put a hedge of protection around you and then use those possessions and resources in you (e.g., skills, talents, education, etc.) or around you to raise you up and out of the abyss of financial distress onto level ground.

The first resource that God used to help the Prophet's widow was her faith. We know that her faith was in God as she sought divine counsel from Elisha—a man of God.

The second resource that God used was her connections. Her husband was one of *the sons of the prophets*—a disciple and servant under the tutelage of Elisha. This connection gave her access to a valuable ally. So, she didn't hesitate to seek Elisha's assistance, support, or advice upon her husband's death and she faithfully obeyed every word of his counsel.

The other resources that God used were a jar of oil and her neighbors' empty jars and bowls. These items seemed insignificant until her faith led her to Elisha, who blessed the oil that God would use and multiply—to produce a financial safety net for her and her sons.

God has a way of assessing our needs, analyzing our resources, and allocating those possessions He will use to bless us financially. For the widow, God used resources she possessed and could quickly obtain to give her the financial freedom she desired. However, her blessings of being able to pay all her debt and then live off the surplus was a by-product of obedience.

If you have a financial need, turn to God in prayer. He may miraculously bless you, but for many of us, it may take a season as God refines us, teaches us, and guides us into His perfect will regarding our finances.

Prayer

Lord, forgive me for not being a better manager of the treasures you have bestowed upon me. You know my financial struggles. Assist me in getting balance and order in my finances, first by helping me be committed to paying my tithes; second by giving me the strength and discipline to spend money modestly until I have paid my debt(s) in full; third by helping me identify simple steps I can take today to improve my financial situation. Turn my deficit into a windfall so that I may be the lender and not the borrower. Remind me often that it is You "who gives [me] power to get wealth" according to Deuteronomy 8:18. In addition, guide me in effectively investing in the lives of others and help me make proper provisions for my family—if I should be called home sooner rather than later. Thank you, Lord, for Your guidance and direction regarding my finances. Thank you for the resources and blessings you have bestowed upon me to help me produce wealth. For I know that "my God shall supply all [my] need according to his riches in glory by Christ Jesus" (Philippians 4:19, emphasis added). Amen.

- PONDER ON -

1. How often do you consider the impact of your financial decisions on your future and loved ones?

....
....
....
....
....

2. What words would your family and friends use to describe how you are with money or how you manage your money, and why?

....
....
....
....
....

3. What financial decisions have you put on hold? Write down some options and decide on a pathway forward (e.g., get professional debt counseling or develop a savings plan to purchase a new home).

....
....
....
....
....

- NOTES -

> Those who trust in their riches will fall,
> but the righteous will thrive like a green leaf.
> ~ Prov. 11:28

Step 10

Being Divine By Design

adorn imperishable beauty

LACK OF SELF-WORTH IS A SPIRITUAL PROBLEM THAT GETS RESOLVED WHEN A PERSON BECOMES AWARE OF HOW VALUABLE THEY ARE TO GOD. SELF-WORTH THAT COMES FROM HAVING A RELATIONSHIP WITH GOD APPRECIATES IN VALUE. IT BRINGS FORTH INNER BEAUTY, WHICH OUTLIVES, OUTSHINES, AND OUTPERFORMS EXTERNAL BEAUTY. IT CARRIES WITH IT THE UNDERSTANDING THAT WE ARE TO TREAT EVERYONE, SELF-INCLUDED, AS IF THEY ARE WORTHY OF GOD'S BEST.

STEP 10

From the Heart of God's Woman

Read: Genesis 12:10-20 and Genesis 20:1-18

Sarah's name means "Princess," she is praised in First Peter for being a beautiful woman, not for her outward appearance but for her attitude toward her husband. Peter says, "Sarah obeyed Abraham, calling him lord …" (1 Peter 3:6).

Let us recapture in our imagination a scene in the life of Sarah, which I envision she handled with the integrity, fluidity, and dignity of a beautiful woman.

Sarah's heart ached with apprehension, but she withheld her anger as she gazed at her husband in awe and disbelief. Her thoughts mumbled, "Hadn't you learned anything from the last mishap in Egypt when we traveled there to flee the severe famine in the land? You have faith in God for an heir, but question whether God will spare your life in Gerar?" Again, she would have to emphasize that she's his sister instead of proudly announcing she's his wife. Sarah doesn't like the situation her husband has put her in once again, but after lovingly confronting him, she accedes with a commitment—to herself—to take the matter to the Lord in prayer.

> *And Abraham journeyed from there to the South, and dwelt between Kadesh and Shur, and stayed in Gerar. Now Abraham said of Sarah his wife, "She is my sister." And Abimelech king of Gerar sent and took Sarah. But God came to Abimelech in a dream by night, and said to him, "Indeed you are a dead man because of the woman whom you have taken, for she is a man's wife." But Abimelech had not come near her; and he said, "Lord, will You slay a righteous nation also? Did he not say to me, 'She is my sister'? And she, even she herself said, 'He is my brother.' In the integrity of my heart and innocence of my hands I have done this." And God said to him in a dream, "Yes, I know that you did this in the integrity of your heart. For I also withheld you from sinning against Me; therefore I did not let you touch her. (Genesis 20:1-6).*

Sarah saw Abraham as having authority over her. Not that Abraham did everything right; as a man of God twice, he brought Sarah into his schemes to save his own flesh, having little regard for the danger he was putting her in. Sarah was so beautiful that Abraham feared that the leaders in Egypt (ref. Genesis 12:10-20) and then Gerar (ref. Genesis 20:1-18) would kill him in an effort to take Sarah for their wife.

Amazingly, Sarah did not question Abraham's integrity, and his mistakes did not prompt her to tell friends and family members about his lapse in judgment each time. She was a princess, in authority over people (Abraham's slaves), and a model of godliness to the slave women. Besides, there were no neighbors to murmur or complain to about Abraham's insensitivity—not that she would. Despite his faults, many people respected him and had come to rely on his leadership. And even though he was wrong, many would have seen her as the problem, not him. Challenging his choice to conceal her identity could reap dire consequences upon her husband. So Sarah trusted God's faithfulness and turned Abraham over to Him. God, being all-knowing, heard her prayers for herself and her husband—and protected them.

There is beauty in having the right attitude and walking in the spirit, just as there is beauty in godly submission. Even though the word *submission* has a negative connotation and can vary in interpretation and application in relationships, the truth is whether it's your husband, employer, or parents, you will most likely find yourself submitting to someone. Yes, there are layers to our submission, just as there are levels to the degree of our voluntariness. A wife wouldn't submit to her employer the same way she would submit to her husband. In the same respect, the extent to which people willingly acquiesce without coercion or undue influence differs. Regardless of the context and nature of our submission, the Bible emphasizes mutual submission. Telling us to be subject to one another out of reverence and fear of God (Ephesians 5:21).

However, submission doesn't give anyone a license to conquer or control another person through intimidation, manipulation, or abuse. Furthermore, the act of submitting shouldn't clash with one's conscience, personal safety, or moral values. The true beauty in submission comes when we love and respect a person enough to seek God's will on how to submit and when to submit in any given situation. Ask yourself: "What would Jesus do?"

Prayer

Lord, "I will praise You, for I am fearfully and wonderfully made; Marvelous are Your works, And that my soul knows very well" (Psalm 139:14). Please help me, Lord, to be submissive to the Holy Spirit within me. Grant me favor with those in authority over me, and give me a willing heart that wants to honor and serve them. Open my eyes and heart; help me to see the beauty within myself. Provide me with a sense of balance in my self-perception and discernment to accurately evaluate my self-worth and whether I put the same concentration and effort into my dress and appearance as I put into developing an intimate relationship with you (which increases my self-worth). I want to be a positive example for others. When I look into the mirror, let me see myself as a reflection of Your goodness and glory. Assist me in being a godly example of beauty and modesty for other women to emulate by showing me what is appropriate or inappropriate for me to wear, do, or say. Thank you, Lord, for being "my light and my salvation" (Psalm 27:1). Amen.

- PONDER ON -

1. What does submission mean to you in a marriage or committed relationship?
....
....
....
....
....
....

2. Do you believe that submission can coexist with equality in a marriage or relationship?
....
....
....
....
....
....

3. What steps can you take in your relationships to ensure that submission, as understood in a biblical context, is applied in a way that promotes love, respect, and well-being for all parties involved?
....
....
....
....
....
....

- NOTES -

> Charm is deceptive, and beauty is fleeting; but a woman who fears the Lord is to be praised. ~ Prov. 31:30

Step 11

Caring for Your Castle

GIVING GRACE REQUIRES US TO HAVE A SUBMISSIVE HEART TO THE WORD AND WILL OF GOD. GRACE TOWARDS OUR LOVED ONES SAYS: "YOU DON'T HAVE TO MEET MY EXPECTATIONS FOR ME TO LOVE YOU; I LOVE YOU FOR WHO YOU ARE." GIVING GRACE IS NEEDED TO MAINTAIN ANY HEALTHY HOME. IT OFFERS LOVE, KINDNESS, FORGIVENESS, COMPASSION, AND SYMPATHY TO ITS OCCUPANTS, WHETHER THEY DESERVE IT OR NOT. IT ALSO REVEALS THE PRESENCE OF GOD IN OUR LIVES.

STEP 11

From the Heart of God's Woman

The Shunammite Woman

Read: 2 King 4:8-37

The Shunammite Woman was a woman of means from Shunem, north of Jerusalem. The Bible refers to her as the Shunammite woman and depicts her as sincere, caring, and hospitable. She was the wife of an older man and, although childless, was very content with her life.

Let us delve back in time into the heart of this woman.

Given the proximity of her home to Jerusalem, it's likely she often encountered travelers heading to and from the city. So when she saw a rather shaggy-looking man walking with a younger man—who looked just as disheveled, she took a keen interest in the pair's wellbeing. She probably chuckled at the younger man's clumsiness, as he often tripped over his feet to stay in stride with the older gentleman, who always seemed to be walking with purpose and intent—forcing the younger man into a moderate jog to keep up.

There was an intensity in the older man's face; she believed him to be a holy man, but it was the gentleness in his eyes that filled her heart with compassion. She assumed they were hungry, so purposed in her heart to venture out and greet them with a meal the next time and every time they passed by her home.

While serving, she developed a deeper, more meaningful relationship with the pair, discovering that the older man's name was Elisha, and his assistant's name was Gehazi.

Although she had catered to many travelers, there was something special about Elisha. When she was in his presence, things seemed brighter, and calmness filled the air. Since preparing meals for Elisha and his assistant, her husband's crops have grown like never before. She probably wondered if Elisha had something to do with their newfound blessings but perhaps dismissed the thought as silly.

On one of their visits, she noticed fatigue in their countenance, so she offered them a place to rest. Later, she would talk to her husband about building a small upper room for Elisha and his assistant to go into and find rest. Her husband, an easy-going gentleman, agreed to her request, and a room was built.

> *And it happened one day that he came there, and he turned into the upper room and lay down there. Then he said to Gehazi his servant, "Call this Shunammite woman." When he had called her, she stood before him. And he said to him, "Say now to her, 'Look, you have been concerned for us with all this care. What can I do for you?...'" She answered, "I dwell among my own people" (2 Kings 4:11-13).*

Despite being childless, the Shunammite woman had a motherly nature, displaying a natural sensitivity to the needs of others. She had the gift of hospitality, opening up her home and heart to strangers and going so far as building a guest room and furnishing it—so the prophet would have a comfortable place to lay his head as he traveled back and forth.

When asked by the prophet what he could do for her in payment for her care and concern, her response was: "I dwell among my own people" (v. 4:13).

Have you ever packaged up your pain and given it to Jesus? Whether the package contains derailed dreams, dead desires, loss of a loved one, physical harm, or any form of suffering and misfortune. To reopen that package would release unbearable pain that only prayer, faith, and your personal relationship with God helped you endure. To progress past the pain, you had to let go of those things that were behind you. So you packaged up your pain and handed it to Jesus, who "heals the brokenhearted and binds up their wounds" (Psalms 147:3). Then you reached forward unto those things which were before you; "[You pressed] toward the goal for the prize of the upward call of God in Christ Jesus" (Philippians 3:13-14, emphasis added).

That must have been how the Shunammite woman felt when asked by the prophet Elisha what could be done to repay her. She expected nothing and asked for nothing. So when the prophet said, "About this time next year you shall embrace a son." Remnants of her packaged pain bellowed: "No, my lord. Man of God, do not lie to your maidservant!" (2 King 4:16).

She had probably come to terms with being unable to bear a child or give her husband an heir, and she decided instead to be a mother in the broad sense of the term—loving and caring for her husband and travelers who passed by her home. And because there was no selfish motivation behind her service, God, through the prophet Elisha, blessed her with the desires of her heart: a child of her own to care for.

Extending grace can win souls for Christ. It can also release unexpected acts of goodwill upon you from God and others.

Prayer

Lord, bless me in the ministration of my home. Grant me the gift of hospitality so anyone invited into my home feels welcomed and cared for. Help me create a home environment that my family members feel honored to come home to, and Your Spirit feels free to roam about. Give me the wisdom to feed my family's mind, body, and soul and to communicate my needs without nagging, whining, or complaining. No one is perfect; therefore, no home will ever be perfect; however, help me to keep my house maintained: the laundry done, the beds made, the refrigerator and cupboards stocked, the dishes washed, and my family nourished. Encourage me so I can encourage my family and others—regardless of whether I get the same encouragement in return. "As iron sharpens iron," let me sharpen the countenance of my family (Proverbs 27:17). If I feel lonely in the daily ministration of my home, reveal yourself as my comforter— reassure me that you will never leave me nor forsake me. Thank you, Lord, for helping me to build a godly domain. May you always feel welcome in my home. Amen. ෴

- PONDER ON -

1. How would you have reacted, given the same situation as the Shunammite woman (i.e., would you have gone out of your way for someone you hardly knew)?

....
....
....
....
....

2. Hebrews 13:2 reminds us: "Do not forget to entertain strangers, for by so doing some have unwittingly entertained angels." How are you sensitive to the needs of those around you?

....
....
....
....
....

3. Think about all the people that you consider hospitable. What specific qualities do they have that make them hospitable?

....
....
....
....
....

- NOTES -

> Above all, love each other deeply, because love covers over a multitude of sins. Offer hospitality to one another without grumbling. ~ 1 Pet. 4:8-9

Conclusion

Keeping God Close

WE HAVE ALL BEEN GUILTY OF NEGLECTING, TAKING ADVANTAGE OF, OR NOT SEEING THE BENEFIT OR MIRACLE IN GOD'S BLESSINGS. IF YOU FEEL DISCOURAGED, DON'T BE. ROMANS 3:23 REMINDS US THAT WE HAVE ALL SINNED AND FALLEN SHORT OF THE GLORY OF GOD. BUT BE OF GOOD COURAGE, OUR ALL-KNOWING AND GRACIOUS GOD SENT HIS SPIRIT—THE HOLY SPIRIT—TO BE OUR GUIDE IN WALKING IN HIS WILL, IN HIS WAYS, AND IN HIS WISDOM.

CONCLUSION

From the Heart of God's Woman

Ruth

Read: Ruth 1:1-22

Bound between Judges and 1 Samuel, *Ruth* is the main character in one of two books in the Bible named after a woman. But who could resist the opportunity to insert a delightful story into a book about love, obedience, and commitment?

Here is a young lady, a Moabite, a descendent of Lot who was Abraham's nephew (Geneses 19:30-38); and in the eyes of most Israelites: a gentile, or put bluntly, a heathen. Yet, in the days when everyone did what was right in their own eyes (see Judges 21:25), God used her to show His people what love is and what love does.

Ruth's love for Naomi was resilient. It had withstood the tragic challenges and hardships of death. The death of her husband, Naomi's son, who died along with his father and his brother in the country of Moab, a land Naomi, her husband (Elimelech), and sons (Mahlon and Chilion) had migrated to, in order to flee famine and possible death in Bethlehem.

Prayer

Most Wonderful Counselor, you are merciful and gracious, full of love and faithfulness. Please reveal to me relationships (with my spouse, children, parents, siblings, friends, coworkers, etc.) that are unhealthy and need transforming. Show me behaviors and attitudes within me that have prevented me from having wholesome relationships. "Give [me] a new heart and put a new spirit in [me]; remove from [me that] heart of stone and give [me] a heart of flesh." (Ezekiel 36:26, emphasis added). As you draw me unto you, mature my ability to love and be loved and to offer support to those in need. Help me build genuine relationships built on love, trust, and commitment. Connect me with like-minded women who love you as much as I do. As Jeremiah asked, I will also ask: "Give [me] shepherds according to [your] heart, who will feed [me] with knowledge and understanding" (Jeremiah 3:15, emphasis added). As I put on the wardrobe of love and compassion, help me be a protective shepherd over my relationships, and thank you, Lord, for renewing my heart. Amen. ৶

- PONDER ON -

1. According to Matthew 22:37-39, what does the "Great Commandment" in the Bible instruct believers to do?

....
....
....
....
....
....

2. What does a strong, healthy, and godly friendship look like to you, and how do you foster it?

....
....
....
....
....
....

3. In what ways do your friends inspire or mentor you in your spiritual, personal, and professional growth? In what ways do you do the same for them?

....
....
....
....
....
....

- NOTES -

> ...as God's chosen people, holy and dearly loved, clothe yourselves with compassion, kindness, humility, gentleness and patience. ~ Col. 3:12

- NOTES -

> Dear friends, let us love one another, for love comes from God. Everyone who loves has been born of God and knows God. ~ 1 John 4:7

www.ingramcontent.com/pod-product-compliance
Lightning Source LLC
Chambersburg PA
CBHW061406160426
42813CB00095B/3487/J